THE GOOD DARK

Ryan Van Winkle was born in New Haven, Connecticut. His debut collection, *Tomorrow, We Will Live Here*, was published by Salt in 2010. His poems have appeared in *The American Poetry Review*, *New Writing Scotland*, *Scotland on Sunday* and Carcanet's *Oxford Poets* series. He has performed the poetry/theatre show *Red, Like Our Room Used to Feel* at Battersea Arts Centre, London Literature Festival and Edinburgh Festival Fringe. He was awarded a Robert Louis Stevenson Fellowship in 2012. He lives in Edinburgh.

ALSO BY RYAN VAN WINKLE

POETRY

Tomorrow, We Will Live Here (Salt Publishing, 2010)
ViewMaster (Stewed Rhubarb, 2014)

RECORDS

Red, Like Our Room Used To Feel (Forest Records, 2012)

The Good Dark
Ryan Van Winkle

To Daisy —
A good dark
for the warm nights,

April 2016
Miami

Penned in the Margins

LONDON

PUBLISHED BY PENNED IN THE MARGINS
Toynbee Studios, 28 Commercial Street, London E1 6AB
www.pennedinthemargins.co.uk

First published 2015

Printed in the United Kingdom by Bell and Bain Ltd, Glasgow

ISBN
978-1-908058-28-7

CONTENTS

ACKNOWLEDGEMENTS

Acknowledgements are due to the editors of the following publications for first printing many of the poems in this collection: *3:AM, The American Poetry Review, Beat the Dust, B O D Y, Gutter, The Istanbul Review, The Ofi Press, Missing Slate, Poetry New Zealand, Poetry Scotland, Valve, The Year of Open Doors* (Cargo Press).

I want to thank the friends and writers who offered their eyes and ears in aid of the work in this collection: Anna Bacciarelli, Krystelle Bamford, Michael Burkard, Dave Coates, Steven Fowler, Colin Fraser, Dan Gorman, Nick Holdstock, Peggy Hughes, Katherine Leyton, Benjamin Morris, Mario Petrucci, Mary Ruefle and Samantha Woods among others (who know who they are and to whom I am equally grateful). Many thanks to Tom Chivers at Penned in the Margins for the care taken in putting this into the world. During the writing of this book, I was Reader in Residence at the Scottish Poetry Library and Edinburgh City Libraries in a post funded by Creative Scotland, I'd like to thank them as well as the following organizations who have offered support in many forms over the years it took to complete this collection: Edinburgh International Book Festival, Highlight Arts, The Robert Louis Stevenson Fellowship and The Scottish Book Trust. I'd especially like to recognize the force for good which is The Forest arts collective in Edinburgh – the artists and volunteers there continue to sustain and amaze me. Thank you to Gareth Warner for his invaluable collaboration on *Red, Like Our Room Used to Feel* where many of these poems were first performed. I am also grateful to Shelley Hastings at Battersea Arts Centre, Deborah Pearson at Forest Fringe, James Runcie at the Southbank Centre, David Stavanger at Woodford Folk Festival and Rupert Thomson at Summerhall for supporting that show. And, of course, thanks to the many friends who have supplied beds, translations and conversations while I've been away from home.

For my brothers

'The place from which you take your orders
is probably the most secret place you have.'
Athol Fugard

The Good Dark

The Duke in Pines

I woke up with Duke Ellington in Pines
like there was nothing else: no muesli, nor porridge,
just Ellington and Pines and so it seemed
I needed to write you a postcard

      telling you *I am okay.* That yes,
it's been a sacrificial three years — but then
I come across the smell of pink soap, pine sap
stuck between cords or a greyhound
snuffing my hand and I think

      I ought to write a long letter that says:
I am doing well. The forest is high
with berries that stain my boots red,
like our room used to feel. And yes,
I am in woods – literal or metaphorical,
you can put me wherever is easy – in a room
where wind always wuthers or in the trunk
of an old, dead tree. I always put you in a dress
you never wore but I used to touch

      every day, getting my shirt or tie
or sometimes I would open the door and look
at the lichen thing, wonder why it had to hang
like an unwatered fern, wonder if it ever wanted you

the way I sometimes wanted you. And, of course,
it was just a dress and it could not say. And I
was just a young man and I could not say,
even about a dress that did nothing but hang.

        I couldn't talk about it. So, what chance
was there for us when I would walk every night
and count one thousand street lamps? If I ever woke
with Ellington and pines you know I would not
wake you to say, would not write it on scrap
paper and leave it for breakfast. I'd just keep
Duke Ellington in Pines in my mind, walk with it,
take it to the pictures, buy it a pop, let it rest on my shoulder
during long journeys. I would smoke Duke Ellington
in Pines with friends and so I am today, smoking
Duke Ellington, wanting to pin him down, write him,
in pines, to you.

§

'How I lived a childhood in snow...'
The Decemberists

All my childhood was snow: summer snow
below the fires of the Forth and September
snow in my bowl, rushed before the bus rose
up a pelted hill.
                    And sometimes I am sure
if you cut me open I would not be recognized
as white, as anything but smoke. Sometimes
all my words were snow and I would push

or pile them in the corner
of my room. I would lie
in bed and watch porn sprout

under snow at the end of the spectrum, snow
so much I forget the names of little flowers

father calls weeds. And still I have
whole years of snow. I return to snow
like a salmon and like salmon I know

the agony of arriving. Is this any way to spend
a day, a life, ploughing snow? Maybe I should
let them be, let the crystals pile high, raise
the roof beams — maybe this week or next
I will place one rare flake in a cigar box,
leave it at your door by way of explanation.

Quarry

Down the pebbled road is a quarry
and, beyond it, a lessening wood
that gets smaller the way toy trucks
and books get smaller as we grow.

I brought almonds to the woods
to give us energy and maybe hope
that if we saw a brown bear by the river
we could feed him our kernels,
look into his eyes and name him.

You said you would name him *Love*.
Watching him try to pull
salmon from a stream
was how you felt before we met
in the damp think of the bar,
your lipstick only wax
the color of a robin I named
in a hurry, the way a stillborn
baby is baptised before it flies,
we hope, blessed
to a kingdom of honey

and breasts. You said, "there are real bears
in Virginia," that we would not find one
here. Then, you ate a handful of almonds
and wouldn't say anything more
about Virginia or what you named
the bears down there. And the next day

it was raining and the next day
they called for a flood. You said
you would call it *Beauty*, the way
the water might send us to our roof,
maybe in the middle of the night.
I'd shiver in my skin, your satin slip
roughed by rain. I asked
if you would be able to catch fish
from the waters that passed and you
looked into my eyes as rain came
like cracks of almonds in a fire
and said, "Yes."

You would surely try. But the hole
trapped the water. The flood never bloomed.

I Do Not Want Rain for Rain

I have known summers
where rain would come cool
as the underside of a pillow. Worms
would leave flooded chambers
and crawl pavement

in a way
we never understood.
We'd pop them on our bikes and
afterwards flick sun-dried skins
against each other.

So, I do not
want rain, for rain
no longer brings the secret
squeak of our shed,
dusty smells

of tomatoes
before they're washed.
Some afternoons the sand would be rain
and wouldn't burn as we placed

our prints,

saw them shrink.
Dad would find a game to quiet us
as the smell of steam seeped into our house.
It was how the trains might have smelled
before oil and electricity,

the smell of a kettle
left boiling: bitter and almost clean.
Indoors was all cardboard and closets
and the sun was not missed
like a brother

who calls to say, "Rain,
I forgive you for holding me
under grey water." I was not always old
and stupid and mean. I was born
innocent. But the sun

made me brutal.
I enjoyed metal handles turned into stove-tops.
When a seat belt burnt my brother on his little hip
he cried so bad we were late for my store.
So I punched him

where he was pink
and he fell on the black, sun-burned tar,
cried till he was told to quit, given an ice-cream
that dripped down his liberty arm.
And now the rain comes daily

like newspapers,
Sunday thick. Not like
a child we welcome home
nor someone dead
whom I welcome

in good dreams
my grandfather takes
my hand, says I am forgiven
for getting to his hospital late,
for the way I speak

to my mother,
for living while he is dead.
And I say thank you and he says to enjoy the rain
while I can. And because he says it, I try.
For when I was a child,

before rain was just rain
or even *God damned rain,* Grandpa was at
the ice-cream bells, calling, "Quick, come quick
before it melts." The grey cloud hanging
in the west pressing closer, pregnant
all over again with rain.

After the Service

It is not compound interest; it is the belief
in compound interest, the reaping we share

or avoid as we accept and deny death.
We think of atoms or protons or quarks;

we count to a trillion with metaphors right round the earth.
But the spring of black mucus does not make a boy believe.

~

The rain comes to wash away snow.
For years Mom kept Gran's lungs

in a box beneath the dogwood tree
only she could see, from the kitchen,

washing dishes, frying a simple egg
that will lay in the belly, get buried there

so solid for a while, forgotten
by the time lunch rolls around. And

when the day comes to unbury her lungs
– I present the lights, Dad's face is a veil,

Peter's shoulders drape. She's soaking salt,
sky black. Snotty clouds pull apart.

~

If she got to heaven, if she went down,
her lamp still on but she's not reading,

she's scratching her chest, Lord knows.
And we found dust, wrote our childish names

with small fingers, put out the lights,
eyes wet with belief.

You May Not Take Me from The Hills, The Sea

The waves were white shoes crashing
down wooden stairs. We took pictures

of night. The hills' tight jeans stretched
over guarded mounds, zipped up lying down.

March your fingers over, push on
organs and seams.

>   Our captain was a boat
>   in a bottle his son couldn't catch.

>   Answers on a high shelf, in the back closet,
>   with the shoebox gun. It has been taken

>   apart and put back together.
>   Here we have only the slant

>   of rain, the smell of oil
>   in the burning dark.

Snow Passing in the Night

What else could it be:
the cool click of heel on tile,
a girl walking her mother,
an old man and coffee cup?
I see it everywhere. My mother
is not next to me.

A purse is clutched
in a freckled hand. I feel it
all the time, like snow
passing in the night, melted by morning.
Someone passes below a bridge
nervous of what might

fall – and I have a bed at home, some kind
of other bridge which I want to be the world.
But my mother is getting old and a girl
is ringing her ankles. The snow is dusting
off the bridge, then going away for a while.

Gerontocracy

I never put my foot down or even tried
to govern and I never pushed a boat out
or offered straw for a poll and my mother
sometimes screamed so loud our neighbours
pretended to water their lawns and my father
would drink so much he'd lose his hearing –
my old man with his channels on yell
and my mother shouting it down. That
was our government and still
I do not think government is evil
or that conspiracy is anything but silence.

Maybe you and I needed bills
like old boys on Capitol Hill; maybe
we needed debate, gavel-bangs, and lashings
of whips. But I couldn't call that government
to order because all I'd ever learned
of government was from Father's hard hand
and all I ever learned of talking
was from the TV; so loud
it spun out everything honest

so I could not tell what was puppet
and what was shadow. So, when my mother
finally took to the lawn and threw her eyes
at her own home I think I understood
the single government of my father
like the night you came home drunk,
your feet wet from the walk, and I spied
your new congress and wished
my own government wasn't owned
by the same old ghosts of old men

who only listen to their lawns,
cash their checks and keep up
till the garage door opens, the engine
turns and we are left with nothing
but noise and the cold majority
of silence below noise.

§

'I think the sea is a useless teacher'
Marie Howe, 'From Nowhere'

How I
looked towards
your eyes as if they
were nothing but waves
and all I learned from the sea
is that it took the sand and never
spoke what it wanted and when we
needed cool it was cool and when we
needed hot it was only a radio signal from
over the sound, coming in weak from Long
Island and when you needed hot you looked in-
to my eyes and said, *Love, your name is darkness*
and I said, *That is not my name, that is the name of my*
teacher, the sea, or a fisherman wishing into waves all night
with his wife keeping the light on then off and all he or I ever
got from the sea was a vocabulary which, like sand, fades and fades.

Wait, Listen, If

If you are reading this
I hope you are going slow,
that the gulls have clasped
their constant beaks. If
the roads are icy, test
the brakes when you are alone,
see if you slide. Leave
the fools and cowboys
to their wreckage.

     WAIT

If you are reading this
it is time to know
that I put the box together.
I folded the cardboard
as if I was inside the box. I know
there were days you wished
me in the box as well.

LISTEN

Once, driving you to school, I forgot
I was taking you to school
and delivered you to work.
The same drive I made daily.
Not because I forgot you were there
but you *being* made me feel
enough like myself to continue.

IF

I could have driven you anywhere
I do not know where we would have gone,
what place at the end of the world
would have been vast and silent enough
for me to take your hand, for me to say —

Window, Not Sky

We dreamed and a bird flew
into our bedroom window

like a heavy book
dropped in the dark.

Not a crack appeared
in your eyes but this lingers

inside me like that dream
when we were in bed and you spoke

with her mouth
at my shivering dick,

saying, "I love you, I know what you love."
Even dreaming I knew this was wrong

but my dick is a simple machine, a straw.
Her mouth was hot as blood

and as you slept she cut me open, smiled

and swallowed so hard I had to pull

your gold hair apart and kiss your cheeks
as if I'd never loved another, as if I knew

you would die.
                    So now I can't fall

back to sleep and wake you up
the slow way in which I'd fix you a bath.

We go outside. The grass is damp and gets caught
between our toes and we find this bird,

his neck broken by clear, sunlit sky –
more like a fish than a bird. His wings

folded behind his back in prayer.
His body below a window
hard as waking, sharp as grass.

§

'It doesn't matter what you know about the other places if you're still stuck in the building.'

David Lynch

My brother phones
and asks only
if I am in the next room.

I am in that room
and the room after that
and outside is a police station,
a bar, a hospital, a hotel. Outside
is a wind that wakes me
from dreaming my brother

calling me from the other room.
And the dream is so like a film
I forget that in this building there is a bedroom,
a bathroom, a kitchen presumably.
In my stirring all I expect to find
are corridors that connect

as a groin connects. And for months
I think about other places
as if I know them as I know my brother.
I think about the bars and even, at times,
the lines on the streets and once or twice
I believe I can depart the building

but I only find corridors – never the hard bush
of the hills or the wind of the valley.
And eventually I will forget other places:
the medicine store, the meat store, the windows of hair-cutters
and I will make an acceptance of here,
of the coins which have left circulation.

And on that day I will not dream my brother
but will speak to you of love for my building
and what I have burnt inside it to stay warm;
what fires I have made of myself and yourself
and the mattress we slept on, the pillow beneath
your back, your forgotten hairs and brushes

and I guess I shall forget you too and the night
when my brother phoned from a dream.
That night I knew you were no longer
in places I could even imagine and therefore

it didn't matter or I didn't matter and I want
a glass of water now

and one hallway that is not a groin,
and a cat to cross my shadow and
there will be a day I'll depart
to all that the world is, I will walk
from asylum like the Indian
in that film where he walks in white
to the end of the reel, towards a fog
he may think
he believes he knows.

I Look Up Again

It has been so long
since I have seen even
a casual moon I forget I can

eclipse the habits of my lifetime,
dust off my boots, walk the craters
and frozen lakes of my skull. If anyone
asked, I'd say yes to orbits and satellites,

would order a main of impact basins and finish
with freeze-dried ice-cream. I would populate the dark
with ghosts of my own and on certain days, stuck down here,
I remember it all – summers burning plastic in woods, night-long
fasts, the smell of mom's hairdresser; wet, singed hair flowered with
alcohol and I know there is no honey or blood and no cheese nor face
begging for a flag and how sad I am when myths wane -- all the chimps,
snakes and sounds went up to drown. If anyone ever asked I'd like to say
yes, somewhere out there, yes, she's a patron of the arts, yes, she pulls,
yes if there is anything but crust and magma I will lift my red nose up
in winter and beg to be told to tide whenever she is swollen and zaftig.
I might cut my hair in slivers, might darn old socks and make time
to walk outside where I can see (but not touch) my lanky breath,

might bake a cake iced gibbous and ready for any ghost
who knocks. They tell me tonight the moon will return

fully dressed in her best gambling gown,
ready to be seen as she truly is;
as I may one day be known
from a distance, in tux

and tails. Tonight, I will
look up. Tonight,
I will look.

The Day Our Desks Grew

I saw it coming when the lights shot on and my friend
went home, so I went too. And on my bed was
a row of ironed Easter eggs and a bag I could fill
with pencils and books. I asked for Joey
but Mother said Joey had school tomorrow, the lake
was over. But it was more than a lake. The creek was over,
the tadpoles and little insects which walk on water.
Like Jesus, Joey said. And Jesus was long since over.
We couldn't find a single skinny bone. Back
before time was something we counted. Before the street lights,
after the street lights – everything changed. Mother
tightened my trousers, slicked my hair and sent me
to the place I'd learn to sit straight, cross my fingers
when I lied. I saw the desks getting bigger and guessed
I was bigger too. And behind the brick building, mounded
in a green dumpster, were all the desks that broke.
Soon to be buried. Not one child among us
who would mourn them or quest to their bones.

Seasoning a Wok

Rub oil and salt into iron with the original
tips of your fingers. Stand as it spits,
as oil seals to metal.

I begin to know new things: how to climb
a hill without sweating, the days it takes
denim to dry, the pressure required to crack a rib.

~

You begin to know old things
at new ages: how your parents
were only playing, how your lover will leave
when she mentions she forgot her wok
back at her old place. Left it,
like it was just another thing, another skin
she'll never retrieve or visit or put near her face,
like brushed cotton just out the dryer.

~

There are things you begin to know

at different ages: the scratch of a mitten
under your shirt or the sound of metal
bending around your car or, today,
how to grow skin, season a wok –
how to bury postcards
from St. Petersberg, Tokyo,
the Florida Keys.

~

I too have sinned, lost things I didn't care for,
thrown rocks, one at a time, at ducks in a pond;
have wrapped crisp meat in pancakes,

have fed myself only
so I'd know new things – how it feels
to buy another pan, how to leave,

how my fingers have nails, how skin
covers skin, how a lost wok sings, seasoned
with a shine of peanut oil and black rice vinegar
so sweet my eyes begin to itch.

§

*'How many times will you do this or that, / without being aware / of the time passing
/ or the time that still remains to you?'*
    Aleksandar Ristović

And it was only a corner
but I turned it with more worry
than normally I worry

as if that corner
was the year of my death
or a shadow of death

which I've dreamed
since I was a child
watching street lamps

dreaming of the day a car would forget
to stop or I'd forget to look. And this
was only a corner, one

of many on a round earth
and the shadows that pass

are only shadows of people

waiting for the lights, checking
their watches or scanning
for an acquaintance

as I dream of my acquaintance
turning up, as if by surprise,
an expected surprise, sure,

as the lights twitch
back to green
after a long red.

A Raincoat, a Spell of Rain Ago

An incompleteness ago:
my fingers and turpentine nails,
laser hairs standing cold.
The market of twilight,
horse left on the monument,
six legs, one raised as a rifle,
his man like an apple in a barn.
          Red on red on red on red.
An incompleteness ago:
a mint melting in the bath, a mint
in pubic hairs and fingered dust,
a mint of dimes, pennies, nickels.
          A quarter a quarter a quarter – call it
an incompleteness ago, a baby almost ate
a banana. Small spoons. Small spoons, small
incompletenesses ago.
The sinks are still buildings,
the counter a revolution,
the gorillas in the kitchen,
the coal train – an incomplete
the bruised boy – an incomplete
the candy shop – an incomplete

the tractor trails – an incomplete, no
incompleteness ago. No grief ago.
No moons ago, no alone ago,
no tires ago, no buzzard pond ago,
no dream ago, no Freud ago,
no pickled vans ago, no cherry ago,
no pits, no canyons, no shaved rocks
of ice from an incompleteness ago.
          No red no red no red no
water for boil, no bottle,
no bottle for punch.
No gum. No shoe.
No shoe detective for my life.
No narrative. No born,
          lived then died.
No tomb, no ash, no clay.
          No bones, no dice
no smoke, no fire. No ants
on the way to mango.
          No incompleteness.
No raincoat for the rat-ta-ta,
          a raincoat ago. A dog ago.
A hat ago. A love ago. A week ago
          there was only no.
No gas. No trucks, only tunnels.

Only pavement. No food, only smell.
No song in my voice.
       No voice.

Epicene

Always covering myself
in clothes or cloaks of words
which only dogs hear: in truth
I was nude and didn't know
which parts to cover or if
I could finally uncover it all.
And what a relief to move
my hands, formally, from
my breasts, testes and labia,
to show myself for what I am –
a worm, or perhaps just a cell
which may birth and split from itself
and I wish you could see
all my secret hairs
revealed like words
or the meanings of words
which always seem concrete
in dreams but never when I wake
and quickly cover.

§

'There is an hour to come when all of us shall cast aside our veils.'
Nathaniel Hawthorne

I'll come back on the hour
our noses change houses
and your veil is no longer a veil.
To think I once called the curtain

a veil, and once I touched
the flesh beneath the cloth
when it was the cloth
I should have touched.

The veil was no window.
The pane and the clouds
beyond the pane will move
from where they are

and come back again
when the birds have changed
the scenery, the sky
and the clouds in the sky –

there is only a blink
when a cloth billows back
to reveal a magician's dove. Pay attention
to the flap of clouds

rushing out to reveal a hole
the shape of the sun.

One Year the Door Will Open

Door, I have knocked, pushed,
licked and, for a year, stroked
your veins smooth as varnish.
My knuckles are hard, black beetles.
      We were children first
      when I saw your blue sway
      into a cottage on the coast.
      Each day the repetitive sea
      sneaking close.
Door, you have been painted many things:
argument red, family yellow, divorce brown.
I too have been locked and pushed
shut, hung on frames and forced to gaze
through creaking day and slamming night
at the parked silver car and children
high on birch. Door, I too have stared
      at my own brass, have become wood
      and squeaked with need. Weathered, pale,
      but still here. So we can peer through gloam
      and into each other, honest as hinge
      and nail, can open and call this home.

§

'Nothing valuable can be lost by taking time.'
Abraham Lincoln

Time is nothingness
and this should allow
me to take any transport

I want. And I will not
hurry in hot haste; nor
will I look to time

as a challenger,
or to you who rushed
to that train

thinking you were late.
The moon was falling,
tripping over your bags,

and I was wanting
to say you were not late,
that the train would come

again and again
like a dream of falling,
like a starfish

regrowing its arms.
And my arms and time
are nothingness and that

should allow you to take
them in your own time,
deliberately, like boarding

a train you know you want,
with a solid name, a destination
stamped on the front.

Summer Nights, Walking

a world quiet as black
and white and warm
as an ironed collar. So,
I want to say sorry

for forgetting to hang
my shirt where my shirt belonged.
You could say I learned something

in the drain of this year,
in coffee grounds, stems
of basil and Chernobyl spewing
all over the radio. That city too

quiet in the summer, full of shadows paused
on garage doors. And tonight I stumbled
into a photo of trees felled in an eye,

all trunk and splinter,
the way your spine dimpled
where it forked. So, I am sorry

for forgetting how love is, how supple
trees bend, how hard hearts break,
how the wind, the snow, the evacuated
rock and chaos.

§

'It was a dark and stormy night'
    Snoopy

It was a dark and stormy night.
The cage was covered
so the bird went to sleep. I switched
the light on, wandered
through the flat house covered
in the dust of a day. Piles
of books lay uncounted and closed
on the carpet among the veins
of maps, the hills I could have climbed
while the sun was open. I counted letters
I should have written on the hill,
the butterfly I might have chased,
locked in a jar, carried home.
For, when the night turned stormy,
I could have said, "I have done
something. I have run
for beauty. I have begun."

~

I could not sleep.
The bird could not sleep.

It was that kind of dark
like a black sheet

drawn over my house.
This is what it feels like

to get older, to lose the veil
of yourself. They say not to look

in a mirror at midnight. You might
find a ghost there,

a future spouse, your killer
looking over your shoulder. I look

at my own eyes. Grey as flags
left on a pole too long. I am sure

I graduated from university. I am sure
I had a favorite cartoon and I know

I watched that video till it bled. I know

I would go home after school. I know

there was Mother's ritual folding
of bread. I know I left home,

drank wine without permission, drank wine
with permission and dropped the glass.

I have dropped more
than I'll ever remember.

I cannot make a list
of the things I've dropped.

It would remind me
to hold. I know I dropped a light bulb

and that I was happy
when a sliver of glass sneaked

so deep into my foot
I could not squeeze it out,

could do nothing
but accept it as mine.

~

I had to meet someone, a shadow
with my face I had to confront.
There was a storm of broken light bulbs, a storm
of lightning bugs in a jar. There were a million storms
I meant to say to myself while the sun was up,
while the mirror was clear. There was a pile of books
to read or burn or bury and a sliver of night in my foot
I needed to remove.

~

I am more water
than I am light.

I feel more for water,
think more about it.

Delicate water.
Hard water.

A tea cup
of water.

A train
of water.

Some say water
has been frozen

and is at rest
in state-sized lakes

on the dark, quiet side
of the moon.

~

It was dark, and stormy. And I
was as visible as anyone, maybe
revealed a little by the rain. But she
began to call me Moon as if
I was far away. *Hey Moon, are you
hungry? C'mere Moon, give us a kiss.*

Later, I became Mr. Moon. *Mr. Moon,
this is serious. We must call a meeting.*

~

This was a dark.
A good dark.
This was a dark dark.
This was end-of-the-reel dark.

This was a varnished dark, a dark hull
on Death's *Ship of Dark* steering north
into a storm grey as old boot lace,
the color of wolf fur and no red
riding anywhere near. His claws
rapped on my window like rain
and begged, so I wrapped
a blanket round my treasures,
tied them to a stick and went
to where I knew a boat was waiting,
its dark sails beating
a hoary breath in the night.

~

I dreamt I was walking with strangers – candles
in jars. When Lennon bit the sky someone said
there are many ways a star can fall. I saw
a woman pushing her eyes into her skull
and did nothing. I saw flies in a mason jar,

languid and plump as raisins stuck in sugar
and I did nothing. I saw light bulbs explode
and stars giving up to gravity and even when
I saw my mother's hand thunder
a jar of peanut butter to the floor
I did not fetch a cloth, sweep up the storm.
I did not dry her palm of blood or hide
the chipped tile from father. I did not look up
long enough to make a wish. I made no wishes.

I saw a boy send his finger into the sky
on the back of a Roman candle.
I walked right up to Mr. Death and asked "How
do you like your lazy boy now?"

~

It was a dark and stormy night. The wine was black.
From the porch I could see waves sharp
as shark fins and everybody was there.
We were always saying goodbye to someone
already gone. And I dropped the bottle
causing a shattered lake on the floor. Much later,
the phone was ringing. They said
it was 1913 calling.

~

It was dark. It was stormy.
It was the beginning.
It was also the middle
and the end. It was four
panels and eight hundred
pages. It was black
and white and full color
on Sunday. It was copied
with Silly Putty, it was burned
for warmth or lined the bird cage.
It softened the package, smelled

like sparklers on the fourth of July –
our names singed into sky, our fingertips blooming
stars till our names were eaten, our sticks sulking
to ash in our hands. Our time of sparks would hasten
would fucking fly
so shake another from the blue box
until the box is empty, until
the storm emerges, until
we we are old enough to write
our names with more permanent fires, burned
onto skin, onto tongue, onto letters on paper

and all, we imagine, longer than sky.

~

It was a dark and stormy night and I listened for a change
in the weather and counted all the pills that had piled up
in jars and plastic bottles – each one a colored star I find myself
wishing upon as I had never wished before. Zinc for libido,
cod liver oil, one-a-day, Vitamin B for the morning after, Vitamin E
for scars and burns, and so many others I collected
without counting.
                    Forgotten children, they sit in the back
of the chest. It was a dark and stormy night and I was counting
all the things that could fall, all the things I could pour,
all the things I could leave behind.

~

Stormy night, she says

and dark, I says

and dark, the parrot says

and dark, she says

and we cover ourselves, make a cage

of blankets. *I like to think*, she says,

that this will be

the end of the world.

Tonight the storm

will rise and swallow

everything which can not

or will not float. This futon

will be our raft, the place

we'd swim to in summer

where parents could only see shapes

and not the point pricking

white skin, hid, water slapping

like tennis balls against the side.

She says she is sad

that this will never be the end of the world

that there will be a tomorrow and the day after tomorrow

until the dark and stormy night when the power went out –

when the light bulb exploded in its socket,

when the parrot learned to say dark,

when we built a cage we understood and which understood us –

will be yesterday and then the day before yesterday and the decade

before this decade when the sheets were smooth, unwrinkled,

light and white as popcorn and the world was ours and ours

alone. She says she can think of ghosts while holding me close,

she says it does not matter that the world is ending, that shadows become monsters, that her thoughts are often haunted

by the man I am not. *The man I am*

enjoys being alone at the end of the world with you, I says

The only thing at the end of the world is the end of the world, she says

And shards, I says

Put your slippers on when you get up, she says,

careful what you step on in the dark.

Dark, the parrot says.

NOTES

The epigraph is from Athol Fugard's interview in the *Paris Review* with Lloyd Richards, issue 111, Summer 1989.

'*How I lived a childhood in snow*' is from The Decemberists' song 'January Hymn' on the album 'The King is Dead' (2010). The poem is also indebted to the work of JD Salinger.

'*I think the sea is a useless teacher*' is from Marie Howe's poem, 'From Nowhere'. This poem is also indebted to Denis Johnson's 'Now' from his collection *The Incognito Lounge* (Carnegie Mellon University Press, 1994).

'Wait, Listen, If' is indebted to This American Life's 'Father's Day' episode (#438) from June 17, 2011. Specifically the fatherly advice: "Slow down and maintain plenty of distance from cars ahead. Let the fools and cowboys roar on to their wreckage."

'*It doesn't matter what you know about the other places if you're still stuck in the building*' is from David Lynch's interview with Kristine McKenna, March 8, 1992. It was cited in Greil Marcus' book of essays, *The Shape of Things to Come: Prophecy and the American Voice* (Picador, 2007; reprinted 2006). The poem is also indebted to Robert Pinsky's poem *The Want Bone* (ECCO Press, 1990) as well as the work of Michael Burkard.

'*There is an hour to come when all of us shall cast aside our veils*' is from Nathaniel Hawthorne's 'The Minister's Black Veil' from *Twice Told Tales* (1837).

'*How many times will you do this or that, / without being aware / of the time passing / or the time that still remains to you?*' is from Aleksandar Ristović's selected poems translated by Charles Simić in *Devil's Lunch* (Faber & Faber, 1999).

14'*Nothing valuable can be lost by taking time*' is from Abraham Lincoln's first inaugural address from March 4, 1861. The full quote reads: 'Nothing valuable can be lost by taking time. If there be an object to *hurry* any of you in hot haste to a step which you would never take *deliberately*, that object will be frustrated by taking time; but no good object can be frustrated by it.'

'The Door Will Open' was commissioned by Rodge Glass, editor of *The Year of Open Doors* (Cargo, 2010), an anthology of new Scottish writing, and the poem is indebted to the spirit of that project and those artists involved.

'Summer Nights, Walking' is indebted to Robert Adam's photography book of the same name (revised edition, Aperture, 2009), and also to Hayden Carruth's *From Snow and Rock, From Chaos* (New Directions Publishing, 1973) and Mario Petrucci's *Heavy Water: a poem for Chernobyl* (Enitharmon Press, 2004).

'*It was a dark and stormy night*' is falsely attributed here to Snoopy (from Charles Schulz's *Peanuts* strip) which mocked the phrase originally written by Edward Bulwer-Lytton in the opening sentence of his 1830 novel *Paul Clifford*. The poem is also indebted to Joy Harjo's 'We must call a meeting' from her collection *In Mad Love and War* (Wesleyan University Press, 1999), E.E. Cummings' 'Buffalo Bill's', Hayden Carruth's 'Quality of Wine' from his collection *Scrambled Eggs & Whiskey* (Copper Canyon Press, 1996), Michael Burkard's 'Talking to a Star' and National Public Radio's story on 'The Armory Show' by Tom Vitale which aired on February 17, 2013.